Mor

BEST WISHES FROM John Dunne

The collected poems of **John Dunne**
Connemara's own

DOON HOUSE PUBLICATIONS

This book is dedicated to the many thousands
of children whose lives were affected by
the Industrial Schools of Ireland

DOON HOUSE PUBLICATIONS
Claddaghduff
Co. Galway
Republic of Ireland
www.doonhousepublications.com
00353(0)95-21180

Ceramic timepieces by Susie Lear,
images of which are used by kind permission
Front cover image: 'The Clock of Life'

Photography Copyright © Ben Crow 2007
Author Photograph: Carmel Lyden

Also by John Dunne:
A CONNEMARA POET
THE MIND OF A POET

Printed in Ireland by Castleprint, Galway
www.castleprint.ie

2 4 6 8 10 9 7 5 3 1

ISBN: 978-0-9556172-0-1

Moments In Time

The Collected Poems of John Dunne – Connemara's Own

THE POEMS

All Things are Temporary	5
The Stillness of Dawn	6
The Sky at Night	7
The Rock and Roll Man	8
Football Galore (The World Cup 2006)	9
The Magic of Arts Week	10
The Joys of Spring	11
Surfing Dudes	12
November Gales	13
The Happy Gardener	14
Horseman of the Night	15
The Bongo Girl	16
Likes and Dislikes	17
Electric Maniacs	18
Egyptian Princess	19
The Mind of a Poet	20
Dancing Flames	21
Christmas Lights	22
A Connemara Sunset	23
The Clock of Life	24
The Bell Tolls	25
Hatchet Man Jack	26
Birds on the Wing	27
Fish and Fishes	28
Weep Not for Me	29
The Oracle of Doom	30
The Discontented Exile	31
My Dreams (You Are My Sanctuary)	32
Faded Dreams	33
Eternal Love Lost	34
Don't Look Back	35
Autumn Leaves	36
A Vase of Flowers	37
Walking My Dog	38
My Doggie Loves the Blues	39
January	40
Hey Satchmo (A Tribute to Louis Armstrong)	41
A Connemara Colleen	42
A Pair of Walking Boots	43

The Jolly Farmer   44
Time and Memories   45
The Elevator Blues   46
The Smoking Ban   47
Standing on the Quayside   48
Pub People   49
Observations   50
Lovers Entwined   51
Anastasia, Girl About Town   52
A Pint of Guinness   53
Moo Cows   54
Saint Patrick The Man   55
Dreamers - Poets - Clowns   56
Crazy People   57
A Winter's Tale   58
The Sky Road Blues   59
Stay Loose - Stay Cool   60
Simplicity   61
Vanity, Vanity   62
We Are What We Are   63
The Journey to Enlightenment   64
Ships That Pass in the Night   65
Pedal To the Metal   66
Nobody Knows Why   67
Johnny Cash   68
Home Is Where the Heart Is   69
Hello - Goodbye   70
Death is Real - Life is Unreal   71
A Game of Pool   72
Andy's Sunflowers   73
A Jealous Mind   74
Cyber Babe Jane 2525 AD   75
Singers and Songs   76
My Infinite Dream   77
Clifden - My Home Town   78
A City Garden   79
The Sea From My Window   80
Inner Beauty   81
Love is a Beautiful Thing   82
The Walk of Enchantment   83
Lost in the Sea of Madness   84
There are Rainbows in the Dark   85
The World of Silence   86
Speak to me of Love   87
If Only   88

About the Poet   **90**
A Letterfrack Boy   **92**

ALL THINGS ARE TEMPORARY

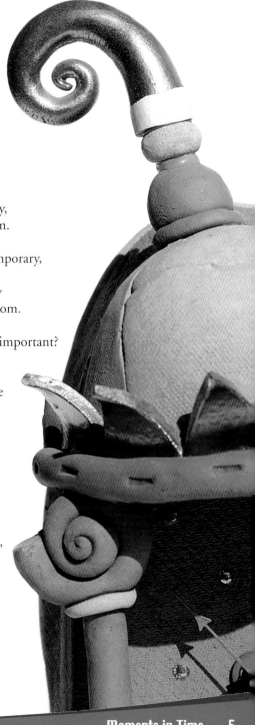

Look inside yourself,
What do you see?
Is it pretty or is it ugly?
Who are you?
What are you?
Whatever you are,
remember this:
All things are temporary.

Your wealth, your poverty,
Your power, your uniform.
It doesn't matter
Because all things are temporary,
We are in transit,
This world is a university
Take your degree in wisdom.

Did you think you were important?
Fool, bloody fool,
Didn't you know
That from dust you came
And to dust
You will return?
It is true. It is.

It is also true that
all things are temporary.

Insofar as you can,
Enjoy your achievements,
In spite of our failings
and indiscretions
We are still the children
of the universe.

We are temporary,
All things are temporary.

THE STILLNESS OF DAWN

Early dawn is a time of peace
A time of stillness.
Misty valleys echo to the sound of singing birds
Newly spun cobwebs glisten in the morning sunlight
And the land is covered in a blanket of dew
There is no wind, not a whisper
Just the stillness of Dawn.

Rabbits scurry to and fro
Trout leap to catch elusive flies
Disturbing the stillness with their splashing noises.
This is a time of magic, a time of wonder,
Nature in all its splendour is laid bare
And I am an intruder
Trespassing on this very private scene.

The sound of grazing animals
Is like no music I have heard before
Feeding, feeding, and feeding
There is an orchestral discipline about them
But without a maestro.
Wildflowers are opening their petals
Eager to receive a
sunny
feast

And hark!
Is that the
wonderful call of the
cuckoo I hear?
Yes it is!

I am indeed humbled,
nay privileged
To be witness to such beauty
I would willingly remain a prisoner
And gladly serve my sentence here in the prison
Of the stillness of dawn.

THE SKY AT NIGHT

Just look up at the night sky
Truly it's an awesome sight,
We are by comparison a tiny speck
Above is a universe of mysteries,
Of wonders, the majesty of it all,
Yes, this spectacle makes me
feel small.

Look at this sea of twinkling stars.
That seems so near and yet so far,
Who then is the architect of this
wondrous plan
Most certainly not you or I,
No, not any earthly being,
but rather,
'One' who is greater than the
universe itself.

It's an ocean, a huge and
mighty sea
Dotted with worlds, known and
unknown.
Quasars, black holes, white dwarfs,
Wow! Does it not frighten you?

Imagine yourself travelling
through the universe
Constantly at the speed of light,
Through the milky way and beyond,
Into the vast unknown,
Into infinity,
Where does it end?
I shall tell you now - it never ends,
Such is the wonder of the
sky at night.

THE ROCK AND ROLL MAN

There he stands, that beast, that animal.
He is the wild creature of rock.
Strutting, jumping and shouting,
Fingers flailing at his guitar.

The fans are screaming
And he loves it,
"Oh baby, baby,
I wanna be with you", he sings.
"We can make sweet music".

I envy him. I hate him,
No I don't.
I want to be him,
I want to be the rock and roll man.

The place is gone mad,
rock, rock, rock,
This guy is belting out song after song,
He is the sultan of rock.
This sweating gyrating monster
Is driving the babes crazy.
Security is working flat out to hold them back.

Are you happy now
Mister rock and roll man?
This is what you wanted
This is what you live for
You are a dinosaur,
An icon of rock,
You are the rock and roll man.

FOOTBALL GALORE
(The World Cup 2006)

Ohlay, Ohlay, Ohlay, it's football galore!
Goals, goals, goals – it's a keeper's nightmare.
Fans screaming, some are dreaming
Maybe their team can win the trophy.

All the big guns are firing,
Brazil, Argentina, Germany, Spain, England,
Come on, Rooney, come on old son,
Put the ball in the net!

Yellow cards, red cards
Oh, what a way to play football poker.
Send him off, ref!
Coaches shouting – some are doubting
It's football galore.

Tackles and diving, how conniving
Corners, free kicks, penalties,
Oh yes – oh no!
One-nil, two-nil, then it's two-one,
I don't believe it, it's the equalizer, two-two!
And the match is drawn.
Joy and sorrow, but there's always tomorrow
And another match to play.

Join the carnival
Enjoy the spectacle
And may the best team win.
It's football galore.

THE MAGIC OF ARTS WEEK

It's great, it's magical,
Full of positive energy
Mount Artistico has erupted,
The artistic lava is flowing
And no-one can stop its thunderous journey.

The place is awash with artists,
Poets, writers, musicians, comedians, dancers
Even clowns ten feet tall
I just hope they don't fall!

Oh the music is fabulous
Jazz, blues, traditional country and rock.
There are side shows with a sprinkling
Of buskers – go on, give them some euros.

Art, art, everywhere.
Try not to miss the exhibitions.
Bring on the clowns, also the jugglers!
Parades for the kids - and fireworks, too.
Bang, boom, bang!

It only happens once a year
So enjoy this artistic spectacle.
Let yourself go, have fun,
The magic flame of Arts Week
Will never be extinguished.

THE JOYS OF SPRING

Spring is in the air
I know, you know.
And so do the birds,
It's a wonderful feeling.

Daffodils can't wait to burst open,
Soon there will be whole legions
Of those yellow sentries
Who only take orders from God.

Spring is breaking out everywhere,
Trees and shrubs with lots of buds,
Are waiting for the 'off'.
And what a race it's going to be.

Nature is blowing its trumpet,
    The ringmaster is shouting
        "Roll up, roll up, roll up folks
            Come and see the greatest show on earth!"

Come and see the joys of spring.
        Running for
        twelve weeks only,
        Don't miss the incredible
        display of colours,
    Listen to all those joyous
songs!

Yes folks,
        Don't miss
            the joys of spring.

SURFING DUDES

They are the cool cats
With surf boards
Under their arms, charging headlong
Into oceanic battle.

The foe beckons those surfing dudes,
It's every surfer for themselves,
Stay on your board, or sink,
No quarter asked or given.

Wet suits glistening in the sunlight,
The shout goes up – let's go
surfing dudes.
They meet the watery enemy head on,
Giant foamy waves
smash into the surfers.

Fight, fight, fight,
you surfing dudes,
Get into the middle
of those circular waves
And surf your way through,
Victory is yours,
you surfing dudes.

NOVEMBER GALES

They blow, they blow,
November gales keep blowing.
Wrap up, cover up, tie everything down,
Because November gales will blow it all away.

November gales are very angry
And bad tempered, mixed with rain
They drive some people insane,
But don't give way to November gales.

Wet and windy, compounded by cross winds,
Opened umbrellas are no defence
Against November gales.
It's so funny to watch the brolly waltz!

Go face into November gales,
Take two steps forward
And four steps backwards – hahaha!
Please don't fall on the pavement.

Are you ready for the challenge?
Right then, in you go,
Charge into the November gales
Get blown about - maybe into orbit.

So be brave,
Join the battle against November gales.

THE HAPPY GARDENER

I think his name is Michael,
But whatever he is called
He sure is one happy gardener.
I just love to sit there and watch him work.

I can tell by his whistling that he is nearby
And, true to form, he soon appears.
I could be wrong
But I think even the birds have joined him in song.

Why do I call him the happy gardener?
I simply don't know.
It occurred to me in a moment of inspiration.
Now, before he starts to work, this Michael chap
Rolls himself a cigarette, lights it up
and surveys the garden.

A huge smile covers his face
And then he sets about his profession.
Weeds start to fly past my ears
And the occasional lump of clay
lands on my lap.
All the while I can hear
the happy gardener.
Because I can't see him now
he is gone in among the flowers.

But not to worry, Michael
soon appears,
His hands covered in dirt
(Why he didn't use a hoe
I shall never know,)
So if you should happen to be
sitting in a public park
Just keep a lookout
for the happy gardener.

HORSEMAN OF THE NIGHT

Horseman of the night
Spurs glinting in the pale moonlight.
Ride horseman, ride.
The night is long,
Your horse is strong,
Ride horseman, ride.

Your business this night is urgent
Many lives depend on you
Do not fail.
Battle lines are drawn.
Sabres unsheathed.
The papers you carry are vital.
Horseman do not fail,
I beg you: do not fail.

The enemy is in pursuit,
They are angry, they are determined,
They want to stop you,
Spur on, horseman.
Speed is in your steed.
You can do it,
Ride, horseman of the night.
Ride like the wind.

Shots ring out,
The smell of cordite
fills the air.
The pain is strong. Ride on.
Horseman ride on,
Camp fires ahead, the front lines.
Stay in the saddle, you're almost there,
Just a little further,
Press on, horseman of the night.
Ride through your lines and to your destiny.

THE BONGO GIRL

She waits, she listens, then
When she's tuned to the beat
She starts to play,
She plays the bongos.
Yeah, she's cool.
She's the bongo girl.

Tap, tap, tap, slowly then
Tap, tap, tap, faster and faster
And faster into a tapping frenzy,
Go, go, go,
Look at the bongo girl go.

The music stops,
But the sound of the bongos
Still echos in our ears.
It's magic,
It's raw energy,
It's wild, it's savage,
It's pure jungle.
The pagan within us is alive.

Bongo girl, what have you done?
We are under your spell,
We are caught in your web
Of mysterious sound.
A whisper in my ear asks,
"Who is she, what's her name?"
I whisper back and say,
She's Rhona, the bongo girl.

LIKES AND DISLIKES

Yes, yes, I do!
I love sugar and spice
And all things nice.
I don't like sour grapes,
I don't like boiled turnips.
Never did.

I like flash cars
But I can't afford one.
Never will.
I like boiled eggs
Too much cholesterol, I'm told.
Will I stop eating them?
No.

I like beautiful women
Yet I can't have them – why?
They tell me I'm too old.
So what?

I don't like weak tea or coffee
It makes me angry,
I don't know why.
I don't like spiders - they are creepy.
I can't help it.

I don't like losing. Does anyone?
I like to win. Don't we all?
I like money. So do you.
I like sunny days,
They make me happy.

So what about you out there,
What are your likes
and dislikes?

ELECTRIC MANIACS

Maniacs, that's what they are!
Downright electric maniacs.
Loud noises at head-banging levels,
Don't they just love it?

Those crazy rock stars with their electric guitars
Revelling in all that delicious sound
Slamming, jamming, jumping, shouting
Like electric maniacs.

They want to control the world, oh brother do they,
Total addiction to rock
Nothing else will do
For those electric maniacs.

Do you know what their language is?
Well, I will tell you anyway,
It's chords and keys and crunching
And more chords.

I know those electric maniacs,
I observe them with detail.
They eat, sleep and drink music,
plugged or unplugged.
That's their scene
and I swear they will live and die
Being electric maniacs.

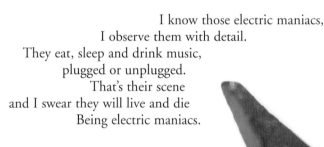

EGYPTIAN PRINCESS

O Goddess of the Nile,
Your beauty is befitting that of a princess.
And truly thou art indeed an Egyptian princess.
My lady, I pledge my life to thee!
My sword shall be your protector,
I will be your champion.

Egyptian princess, I will build you a pyramid
Greater than that of the Pharaohs,
Be it of gold or silver it matters not.
Your wish is my command,
And it shall be built my princess,
On my solemn oath, it shall be built.

Lady of beauty
Thou hast captivated my mind, my heart, my soul.
You are the heat that keeps me warm in this world of winter.
Show me thine enemies and I will slay them all,
Their blood will moisten the dry desert sands.

Even Ra Moon can not compare with thee,
My beautiful Egyptian princess.
The gods have declared you royal
And as such are worthy of all homage.

Ask of me what thou will,
For I am your servant.
Egyptian Princess,
I cast myself at your feet!

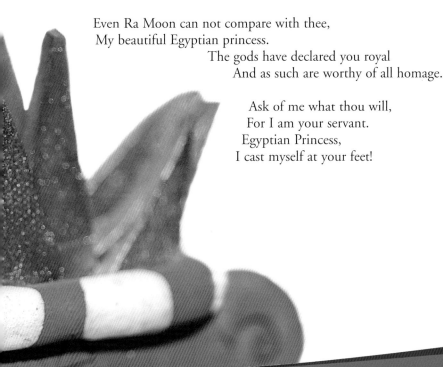

THE MIND OF A POET

How does a poet think?
Why does a poet have to express
The thoughts that pass through his mind?
What compels this painter of words to sit,
To think, then to write down those ideas
And notions arrived at?

Poets receive and transmit messages.
Signals can be strong or weak,
Depending on their state of mind.
Each poet has his own style,
Different in method and presentation.
Some can be angry, funny, even romantic,
Others will touch on the political.

The mind of a poet is complex.
It belongs to the family of art;
Poets paint invisible pictures,
Their works hang in unseen galleries.
And yet, those creations excite, inspire,
They lift up the spirit of man.

The wind blowing across desolate places
Is music to the mind of the poet.
The sound of the ocean sweeping ashore
On still nights.
I long to translate that sweet noise,
I want to describe the setting sun
So golden and beautiful.
Everything I see and hear inspires me.

My mind tells my heart what to say
And so it is that poetry flows.
This is the mind of a poet.

DANCING FLAMES

Gaze into a blazing fire,
Now tell me, what do you see
Dancing flames, that's what you see,
Crazy dancing flames.

They have names, you know,
Oh yes, they do.
Well there's Dancing Jack,
Flaming Mick, and Hot Coals Tom.
There's a whole troupe of them.

Have you noticed
That they never stop dancing?
I guess why that's why they're called
dancing flames
They want to capture your mind.

Try and get to know the dancing flames
They can take you to a world
Where your imagination runs riot,
It's a fantastic experience.

So, don't delay,
And do try to make friends
With the dancing flames
They're just
flaming
magic.

CHRISTMAS LIGHTS

Christmas lights are shining
Bright and clear
They are winking at you and me,
Throughout the world
Christmas lights are glowing.

Christmas lights are telling us
It's yuletide, it's time to unite,
There's shelter for all at the inn,
Let's be as one on Christmas night.

Do your shopping, enjoy the fun,
But, before you run,
Please stop and look
At the Christmas lights.

Let the Christmas bells ring out,
Be of good cheer
May there be peace and
goodwill on earth
And let Christmas
lights shine.
Merry Christmas, everyone.

A CONNEMARA SUNSET

It is magical
It is awesome
It is spiritually uplifting
To observe that golden globe
Descending beneath the Connemara skyline.

A spectacle indeed,
A truly magical display
Of nature's glorious might,
And yet, a Connemara sunset
Is a gentle affair.

The seas become calm,
The clouds disperse,
Evening has fallen across the land,
And so the stage is set
For the main event.

Slowly, but surely,
That golden orb
Drops beneath the distant ocean.
It is not angry
But rather benign.

My description
Cannot do it justice.
So please come and witness
for yourself
A Connemara sunset.

THE CLOCK OF LIFE

Tick tock, tick tock,
The clock of life ticks on.
Every beat of your throbbing heart
Is a second gone.

Live my darling, live life to the full,
As you have done and will do.
Drink of the wine of life,
And may your chalice be always full.

Live life, live, live life,
Because time and tide wait for no man
Listen to the clock of life.

Tick tock, tick tock.
Time is passing by,
So hurry, be daring, be brave,
Live before you die.

THE BELL TOLLS

Dong! Dong! Dong! and so the bell tolls
But for whom does it toll?
Is it for thee or is it for me?
Dong! Dong! Dong! the bell tolls.

Listen to the bell, it is speaking to us
Do we understand the message?
The bell speaks many languages
Dong! Dong! Dong!
Yours is different from mine, or is it?
No, it can't be tolling for me
It must be tolling for him, them, or her,
But surely not for me.
Ah, but the bell knows for whom it tolls
Dong! Dong! Dong!

This is silly man, it's only a bell
And anyway, bells are always tolling
For one thing or another.
I agree with you, sir,
I agree with you whole heartedly!
But this is not just any bell,
The bell that tolls now
Is the bell of Eternity.
Dong! Dong! Dong!

No it can't be tolling for me -
no I've been good!
Why, only the other day I gave alms
to the poor!
It's on record you know, yes it is,
I think the bell tolls for them
over there,
They're bad you know, real bad.
Dong! Dong! Dong!

Who then does the bell toll for?
Dong! Dong! Dong!
The bell tolls for humanity.

HATCHET MAN JACK

They seek him here, they seek him there,
They seek hatchet man Jack everywhere.
He is brazen and daring,
Look at his eyes, wild and staring.

His laughter is loud and chilling,
Hatchet man Jack is so scary,
Watch out for him, because he is lurking,
Waiting to catch the unwary.

Listen out for Jack's footsteps,
They echo with menace, boom, boom, boom.
The ground beneath him trembles,
With his hatchet gleaming, Jack is relentless.

Hatchet man Jack is broad and tall,
With his long strides.
He will soon be upon you so run, run, run.
Run from that crazy man.

Run from hatchet man Jack.

BIRDS ON THE WING

Fly, fly, you beautiful birds on the wing,
You have no cares
Just fly and feed yourselves
With berries and worms, Nature's fare.

Such simplicity, such magic,
I could watch you for hours,
And listen to your singing – it is heavenly,
That's the Lord's gift to you.

The dawn chorus,
It's just oh so glorious,
None of the composers could ever write such music,
And that's a fact.

Birds on the wing,
I wish I could fly like you,
Fly away across continents and oceans,
But mortals cannot grow wings.

Freedom is only for you
birds on the wing.

FISH AND FISHES

I go fishing and catch fish,
Maybe one, two or three,
But when there are four or more
I'm tempted to call them fishes!
So it's a contest between 'fish' and 'fishes'.

Some fish don't want to be left behind
If I land one, the other fishes
Jump up and say, "What about me?"
I shout back and say, "Don't worry, I can see!"
I'm thrashing, the fish are splashing
The whole scene is very fishy indeed!
None of them wants to wait its turn
And my reel is about to burn.

Plan B comes to mind,
Catch and throw back, catch
and throw back,
Faster and faster!
Finally it dawns on me
This is how fish and fishes get their fun!
So what do I do?
I quickly pack up my gear and run
Leaving the fish and fishes behind!

The next time I won't be so blind,
I promise you.

WEEP NOT FOR ME

If you pass my way and I am dressed in rags,
Weep not for me for I have known riches
And have had my share of fine things.
I worshipped at the shrine of wealth
And mocked my lesser fellows.
I gathered round me the coins of greed.

Foolish me, fool's gold, false happiness!
I laughed and danced in those places of merriment,
I drank the wine and had some more,
The world was at my feet.
Disaster was never a possibility.
It was life in the fast lane - zoom! zoom!

My addictions overcame me, I became reckless
Drove fast cars, squandered my wealth;
Now alas, I am down and out,
I beg for my living.
But do not weep for me for I am at fault,
I will not begrudge others that which I have lost.

Look at me and say:
"There but for the grace of God, go I."
Perhaps I shall rise again from the ashes of despair,
But for now I must wander the streets
And parks of this city.

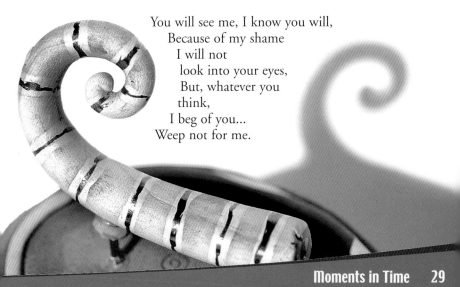

You will see me, I know you will,
Because of my shame
I will not
look into your eyes,
But, whatever you
think,
I beg of you...
Weep not for me.

THE ORACLE OF DOOM

Master of the Oracle, spare me this vision,
I beg of you, let this chalice pass from me,
I do not wish to witness such death and destruction.
Why must I be the recipient of this terrible thing?

"I am the Master of the Oracle
and I command you now,
Gaze into its depths,
Tell me what do thine eyes see?"
Yes! my master, I see and I tremble,
I ask you again master, spare me this vision.
"Silence I say!
You are the servant of the Oracle,
And I am the master!
Once more I command you to cast your eyes
Into the Oracle of Doom.
Now servant, speak, reveal the vision in the oracle."

My master, I see hideous demons
Mounted on steeds of fire,
They ride by night across the land
Through towns and villages,
Their swords crimson
with the blood of many,
There is much wailing
and sorrow.

"Tell them servant, tell them all,
What thou hast seen
in the Oracle of Doom.
Tell them it will come to pass
Because they do not know
The day of visitation."

THE DISCONTENTED EXILE

I left so many years ago.
Yes, I left my native land, the place that I loved,
With each year that passes
I yearn with all my heart to return.
With each short visit
My yearning grows stronger and stronger.

Now I know that I must return,
Return to that land I had to leave.
I can no longer stand the pain of exile,
My mind, my soul, my heart,
Cries out in anguish;
I am truly a discontented exile.
In my troubled sleep I hear voices saying
"Come back to Erin,
Return to the land that gave you life."

In my dreams I see the green fields,
I see mountains that beckon me,
"Come back," they say,
"Come back to us."
I see waves sweeping onto beaches,
The beaches of my childhood,
I once stood upon those white sands,
And looked out across churning seas.
They echo and echo "Come back to
Erin, my son.
Come back to Erin,
Do you not hear us calling you?"

MY DREAMS!
(You are my sanctuary)

My dreams, my dreams you are my sanctuary,
You are my substance,
You shield me from that which I cannot face:
This vulgar world.
I shudder at the thought of it,
Without my dreams I would be lost,
Lost in a sea of fear.

My dreams, my dreams, you are my sanctuary.
Take me into your embrace,
Shield me from tomorrow and its reality,
Its daunting prospects,
All that is hidden is bliss.
Decisions are the lot of others,
But not I, no, not I.

My dreams, my dreams, you are my sanctuary,
I seek solace in you, my dreams,
I love to wander down your dreamy byways
To rest beneath your trees of happiness
And seek contentment.
Only in you, my dreams,
Can this be found.

FADED DREAMS

Discard your faded dreams
And yesterday's memories.
Why burden yourself
with events
That did or did not happen?

Do not fret if love has
passed you by,
For there is much virtue in loneliness.
Enjoy your singularity,
With its many flirtations,
Others will envy this freedom.

Walk your daily walk,
And if you should see children play,
Remember that once you were they.
Young dreamers, wanting to be many things,
I say act them out or they will fade away.

You will have money, or maybe you won't,
Either way you will spend it.
There is a certain attraction to those coins and paper.
Some say it comes easy and goes easy, it's up to you.
But do be cautious in your business affairs.
The sun will shine,
Rain will fall – that is certain.
What is not certain is how humanity will destroy itself.

But do not dwell upon such calamities
Because, in spite of your faded dreams,
The love you nearly had, but didn't,
The horses you backed which won or lost,
Your success and failures,
In spite of everything,
It is still a wonderful life.

ETERNAL LOVE LOST

I knew thee well, sweet eternal love
I knew thee well,
But alas, I lost you,
With much regret I lost you.
I once embraced you whole heartedly
But now in my shame
I avoid your calling.

In my youthful innocence, I thought you were
The fountain of all knowledge,
How very foolish of me!
But then, I could not see,
I was blinded by your glow,
I abandoned the ability to think,
I was not aware of other wisdoms.

Eternal love, I lost you, I know,
But will I find you again?
Perhaps I shall,
And then again, maybe not.

You see, eternal love,
The gods look with favour on some,
And others they punish.
It could be that my lot is to wander
Forever in the sea of heartbreak.

Where shall I find solace?
Save me, eternal love.
Do not abandon me.

DON'T LOOK BACK

Please don't look back.
It's gone,
It's gone, it's over.
Memories still linger,
The hurt remains with the pain.

Don't look back now
And ask:
What was said by who
To whom, and why?
Leave it, leave it, let it rest!
That is the way things are.

Oh, love is cruel,
Love is kind.
Love can also be blind,
Love takes no prisoners.
Wounds received in the battle of emotions
Take time to heal.

Don't look back
What good will it do?
What's done is done.
Shed your tears,
Bite your lip,
Wreck all around you (if you must)
But don't look back.

Go forward,
Forward to the future and
Remember this,
Don't look back.

AUTUMN LEAVES

Autumn leaves are brown,
Dry and weary,
With strong winds blowing.
Autumn leaves are falling down.

Not long ago they were green
And handsome, proud and strong,
Now their season has come and gone,
Autumn leaves will just be swept along.

Chestnut and ash, willow and maple,
I'm sorry to say, you have become wasted.
It's like old age, it happens to us all,
I guess they call it the big fall.

But through spring and summer
There is reincarnation, you will be new creations
And in the autumn
Your fate is to become autumn leaves.

Goodbye, autumn leaves.

A VASE OF FLOWERS

How pretty, how simple they look,
With their stems bathed in
crystal clear water.
They look so radiant and happy.
A far cry, of course, from their origins.

Soft gentle flowers, where did you
come from?
What lovely place were you born?
Was it some windswept bogland?
I suspect you were at the mercy of
Mother Nature,
Tossed and flung about.

Sweet flowers, now you are safe
From all danger, safe in your glass vase.
See how tall you and your
fellow flowers stand.
I wouldn't be surprised
If someone made a painting of you.
If I could, I would.

I just want to sit and stare at you,
It's so pleasant and relaxing.
I adore your beauty,
I want to reach out and touch
your soft petals.
I'm not crazy, just plain happy,
To do justice to a beautiful
Vase of flowers.

WALKING MY DOG

Walking my dog is not a bad job,
Some say it's a slog,
But think of it as a jog.
So off I go with my dog
On extended leash.

Woof, woof, to other dogs.
Growl, growl at pussy cats along the way,
Lamp posts are watered,
Car wheels get drowned.
Hey, I'm just walking my dog!

Passers-by ask, what's your dog's name?
I say Bonzo.
My hound doesn't like it
Because he's one of those
macho beasts,
One of his ears stands up,
the other doesn't.
I don't know why.

A frog jumps out in front of us,
My dog goes ape,
But he can't escape,
He barks, he growls and cries,
all at once.
Then runs off at high speed,
On a long lead.

Walking my dog keeps me fit,
Though afterwards I'm dying to sit.
My dog is a lovely creature
And his loyalty is his best feature
Yes, folks, I just love
walking my dog.

MY DOGGIE LOVES THE BLUES

Yeah, my doggie loves the blues,
He howls when he hears those notes,
Wooo, wooo, wooo.
I ask him what he's saying
and he says:
Sure done love those blues,
Wooo, wooo, wooo!

I don't know when it all started,
And I must say I find it
very strange indeed,
But it's true, you know,
That my doggie loves the blues.
Come on doggie,
Let's hear you howl those blues,
Wooo, wooo, wooo!

My doggie ain't no crazy animal
And I kind of like the way he swaggers,
But if he hears a blues song he just goes wild,
Yes, folks, there's no holding him back,
And don't say I didn't warn you,
Because my doggie loves the blues,
Wooo, wooo, wooo!

Now if you should see me walking my dog,
Just stop and say to him,
"Hello doggie, I hear people say you like the blues!"
But don't be surprised if he turns and says
Yeah, man you're doggone right,
I sure do love the blues, wooo, wooo, wooo,
I sure do love the blues.

JANUARY

Christmas is gone, money all spent,
And we are coming into January – how awful!
All you can do is wait for something else to come along.
Suggestion: try hibernation.

January is so bland, so boring.
January is long and wet and cold.
"Will it ever end?" I say to my friends – they say
"Of course it will, you silly billy."

The trees are so bare, it's like having no clothes on.
But the birds don't seem to care,
They keep on singing regardless.
I bet our feathered friends could migrate.

So what can we do about January?
Well, you can play cards, drink beer
Watch football, bite your nails,
go to sleep.
And when you wake up –
January should be over.

HEY SATCHMO
(A tribute to Louis Armstrong)

Hey Satchmo,
  I like your gravel voice and cool lyrics.
    And so you knew 'Mack the Knife'
    And said hello to 'Dolly'.

    Hey Satchmo,
     Let's hear you play that
     Trumpet of yours and sing
     'It's a Wonderful World'.

    Hey Satchmo,
   Thanks for all your music
  And fun, yeah Satchmo,
You really did make it a wonderful world.

A CONNEMARA COLLEEN

She is a real Connemara colleen alright,
With her laughing eyes
And cheeky smile,
Exposing pearly white teeth.

She has a beauty, a lot of beauty,
And when she winks,
There's mischief in her eyes,
So watch out!

This Connemara colleen has spirit
And a sharp mind,
Trade words with her
And you will come unstuck.

She is funny, she is lively,
And loves the outdoor pursuits,
Comes from island stock, you know.
Oh yes, she does!

I bet this Connemara colleen
Can row a currach
With the best of them
Yes, and cast a net as well.

With her flowing hair
and proud walk
She is a thoroughbred
with a lot of class.
Quite simply, she is,
A real Connemara colleen.

A PAIR OF WALKING BOOTS

We are a pair of walking boots
And don't we get a lot of punishment?
Only today our owner brought us down
This really awful rough road,
And do you know what?
There were rocks the size of boulders.

Ouch! Watch it, owner,
You've nearly broken the pair of us boots!
Good God! What's that in front of us?
Oh no, it's a puddle!
That's not a puddle mate,
That's a lake, that's what it is!
And we have to go through that
But we can't swim!
Listen you leather 'Wally'
We boots don't swim, we just walk or run.

Where are we going now?
Well, it's over a wall and across some fields.
We hate going across fields,
We might step into some of the cow stuff,
You know what I mean.
Speaking of which, you have just gone
And stepped into the stuff - damn!
Now it's going to take miles of walking
To get rid of it.

We boots get around, don't we?
Up hills, down dales, across mountains
And fields, river beds and so on.
Did I mention that my boot-mate and I
Once walked across the Alps? Honestly,
Ask our owner Susan!
She will tell you that we are her pair
Of walking boots.

THE JOLLY FARMER

Hello, I'm the Jolly Farmer.
I ain't no charmer, am I?
I mean, look at me!
Wellies covered in cow dung,
And it doesn't half pong, ha! ha!
They call me the Jolly Farmer.

I've got lots of land you know,
Yeah, acres of it, well, look around you.
There is enough here for a zoo,
Except I've got cows and sheep.
They never stop bleating
Where's my dog, I'll sort them out!

There's my tractor over there,
It's had lots of wear,
But I don't care!
Hell, I'm the Jolly Farmer.

Look at all those chickens,
They had better lay me
some eggs
Or they will be finger lickin'.
Yes, folks,
I'm the Jolly Farmer
Ha! Ha! Ha!
I'm the Jolly Farmer

TIME AND MEMORIES

Fond memories, sad memories, glad memories,
Though some may last, others will pass.
These are the substance of time and memories,
Recollect,
Forget accordingly,
Tiny capsules of life, prescribed by a deity
Greater than you or I,
Do not question,
Just ride the train of time and memories.

Laughter, gaiety, mirth,
Yes! Oh the fun of hours in the sun.
Time flew by,
Why was I too shy to say goodbye?
Regrets? No, no, never.
I was never that clever.

Sad memories?
Yes of course.
Without recourse to remorse.
Friends lost at what cost?
Arguments settled, some unsettled.
Sad, but never got mad,
Always rationalised,
Patience is a virtue few have in abundance.

Glad memories?
Yes,
Oh yes,
Of girls kissed,
Romances missed - oh my!
How sweet to reminisce,
Thoughts of lovers, past and present
Fill my mind,
No time, to waste,
Must move on,
Tick, tock, the clock of life ticks on,
Hurry, hurry all aboard, catch the train
Of time and memories.

Sad memories?
Yes, of course.
With recourse to remorse, friends lost, at what cost?
Arguments settled?
Some unsettled,
Sad but never got mad.
Always rationalised.
Patience is a virtue that few have in abundance.

THE ELEVATOR BLUES

An elevator goes up and down,
So do the blues.
One day you're up, the next you're down.
My guess is you've got the elevator blues.

Friday, Saturday, Sunday, you're high,
Monday, Tuesday, Wednesday and Thursday you're low.
It's an equation with no explanation.
It all equals the elevator blues.

Birds and bees don't get the blues,
They haven't got the time.
Cats chase mice, but not in elevators,
And that leaves us, the usual suspects,
Yeah, we're guilty of the elevator blues.

Got the blues? The remedy is this.
Jump into an elevator,
Go up and down, up and down,
Now sing out, 'I've got the elevator blues,
Oh, yeah, I've got the elevator blues!'

PS: Tell me if it cures the blues.

THE SMOKING BAN

It's no joke, mate.
No more smoking in public places.
Dying for a puff, hahaha!
Sorry, but you can't blow smoke
In people's faces.

But I'm desperate for a fag,
Oh please, please, I need a drag,
Run outside, light up if you can,
Because it's all down to the smoking ban.

The wind and rain will put your light out,
Now you will have to shelter in pain.
Why must I smoke?
Maybe it's because I'm just a dope.

Give it up, old son!

Or perhaps you can't.
So what can I do?
Well you can go on smoking,
But do remember, there's a smoking ban.

This is crazy, this is madness,
I must have my cigarette,
Hey, that's fine, that's okay,
But don't forget the smoking ban.

Yeah, don't forget the smoking ban.

STANDING ON THE QUAYSIDE

I am standing on the quayside,
There is hustle and bustle all around me,
Boats loading and unloading,
Crewmen joking with each other,
The smell of freshly caught fish is strong,
Boxes and boxes on the quayside
Bound for some market.

The seagulls flying overhead
Are screaming their hearts out,
Looking for a bite to eat, I suppose.
Vans, cars, jeeps, keep coming and going,
But not one of them had to beep.
There is order and urgency.

The sea is calm, a slight swell perhaps,
But quite sedate.
People are boarding different vessels.
There are hikers, bikers, and fishermen
With high expectations.
Lovers are much in evidence,
All of them off to the islands for the weekend.

I won't join them. No!
I would rather stand here on the quayside
And bid them all a bon voyage.

PUB PEOPLE

Some are quiet, some are loud
And others just stand about drinking.
But they all have one thing in common,
They are pub people.

So who are these pub people?
Well, there's rich, poor and not so poor,
Farmers, fishermen and builders,
A sprinkling of pensioners enjoying a tipple or two.

Banter flows with the beer,
Jokes good and bad are told.
Why do white sheep eat more grass than black sheep?
Because there are more of them!
Someone shouts, hahaha!

It's fun watching and listening to pub people.
Who needs TV?
'Pub People' is a much better show.
        And it's also live.

                So do come and join the pub people,
                    Have a laugh, just relax, let it happen.
                        I ask you, one and all, to raise your glasses
                            And say 'cheers!' to pub people.

OBSERVATIONS

Think of observations as photographs
And your eyes are the camera:
CLICK
A robin, perching on a branch,
Calling its mate,
Cheeky thing.
CLICK
The musical sound of a running stream
Ending in the roaring crescendo of a waterfall
Pure magic.
CLICK
An elderly man sitting on a bar stool
Drinking his pint, happy in his retirement.
How nice for him after a lifetime of work.
CLICK
The laughter from children as they play,
So refreshing.
CLICK
A loving couple lost in each other's arms,
How beautiful and romantic.
CLICK
Observations are a wonderful pastime,
All of life is there to be observed.
CLICK
A pretty woman walking by
gets me all hot and bothered,
Yeah, well, that's the way it is.
CLICK
A yacht sailing out to sea,
Excitement and adventure.
CLICK
The setting sun and day's end,
How peaceful.

And tomorrow there will be
many more observations.

LOVERS ENTWINED

How beautiful they are, these young lovers.
Eyes looking into eyes,
Bliss, bliss, lovers' bliss,
All sealed with a lingering kiss.
Lovers entwined, hearts combined,
  The world does not matter,
    Love has dominion over all.

        If one could harness the power of love,
          The world would be bathed in light,
            Evil would take flight.
              God of love, spare these lovers,
                Give them the power of eternal love.
                  Look at them, are they not so sweet?
                  Love is strong, so powerful.

              Lovers entwined I envy you so,
                With your clasped hands and
                  sparkling eyes,
                    Spoken tender words with one
                      understanding,
                        You are truly lovers entwined.
                        Remain so, dear lovers, always
                        remain so,
                          Show love for all to see.
                            Lovers entwined, I love you.

ANASTASIA GIRL ABOUT TOWN

Hey, Anastasia, where do you go?
What do you know?
I see you walking, see you talking,
Anastasia, girl about town, come and sit down.

So, Anastasia, are you clubbing, even pubbing?
Why do I ask? Just curious I guess,
Haven't seen you lately, I like your energy,
That's your attraction, it gives me much satisfaction.

Are you talented, my dear Anastasia?
Do you sing or dance or maybe rock and roll?
Perhaps you're a writer, mysteries, thrillers, murder, romance,
Whatever, one thing is certain – you're so cool.

Am I an admirer, even a suitor?
No, no, beautiful, lively Anastasia,
Just an observer, and not very clever,
I adore humanity with all its frailties,

But, Anastasia, girl about town,
You're so special.
Be eccentric, be different,
Dress to please, dress to tease,
Be Anastasia, girl about town.

A PINT OF GUINNESS

A work of art,
That's what a pint of Guinness is!
Liquid gold, black nectar.

Food in a glass,
With lots of body,
(Thou hast more flavour
Than a scented rose).

A pint of Guinness is medicinal
With lots of vitamin D
That's what it contains.
"Get it down you, mate!"

Beverage divine!
Beverage supreme!
(Thou art indeed king)
And, ladies and gentlemen,
In case you didn't know,
The plural of Guinness is...
Guinni!

moo cows

Cows say, "Moo!"
And I say, "How do you do?"
Cows chew grass, give us milk,
Just try drinking it from a glass.

Have you ever heard moo cows singing?
Well, it's called 'Looing',
There are high loos and low loos.
Lots of mooing, with a bit of chewing.

The male cow is knowing mister bull
His job is to keep
all the moo cows in check.
I bet his life never gets dull!
Increase and multiply,
He lives life to the full.

Butter, cheese, dairy spreads,
All come from moo cow herds.
So, my good people, be kind to moo cows.
They always deliver the goods,
Without them
there would not be so many foods.

In parting, I just want to say
A big thank-you to all the moo cows.
Moo, moo. MOO!

SAINT PATRICK THE MAN

He is the man,
The man who brought
Christianity to Ireland.

He is the man who walked
The length and breadth of this land
To bring us the word of God.

He is the man who fasted
On a mountain top, he is the man
Who turned us from our pagan ways.

He came to us as a boy
Left as a man, and returned again
As a bishop.

He is the man who gave us new life,
Gave us meaning; Saint Patrick
With all our hearts we honour you.

Saint Patrick,
you are
the man.

DREAMERS – POETS – CLOWNS

DREAMERS

Dreamers dream of many things.
Dreamers dream of greatness,
Wanting to be,
But never being,
That which they dream of.

Generals at war,
Masters of sport,
Rich and famous,
Lovers in movies.
These are the
dreams of dreamers.
But do not despair,
Because sometimes
dreams come true.

POETS

Poets write, poets sing,
Poets hope that people are listening.
Words, words like sweets in a jar,
There are lots of them.
Pick one of those words
and undo the wrapper,
Now, reveal the poet's message.

Poets protest in their writings,
They speak in a way others will not.
They are carpenters,
They are painters,
They are sculptors.
They are all things.
So please – do not slay the poets.

CLOWNS

Do bring on the clowns
They are funny, funny, so funny.
Listen to the children's laughter
As they watch the clowns' painted faces,
They scream with delight
As the clowns fall about.
Tricks, tricks and more tricks,
Pranks, smoke and bangs,
Hurrah for the clowns.
They are wonderful,
They are magnificent.

Just tell me this:
Who will console the clowns?
Because we are all dreamers, poets and clowns.

CRAZY PEOPLE

They are great
They are mad
They are wonderful.

Crazy people shout, scream, laugh.
They are the soul of life
In pubs, at parties,
They deliver the fun.

A gathering of crazy people
Is like a mad hatter's tea party.
Who will sing first?
They all will.

I love these crazy people.
Why do I love them, why?
Because I am one of those people,
Yes, I am one of those
Fantastic, funny, crazy people.

A WINTER'S TALE

Gales, gales, rain and hail all combine
To make a winter's tale.
Snow and Jack Frost are certainly our lot,
So wrap up and keep warm,
Because the winter is long and dreary.

I see a little red robin perching on a naked branch,
It must be very hungry,
And I wonder how all of them manage,
Nature provides for them, I guess.
And I'm sure there are berries nearby.

The world of winter is so bland, so dull, so boring,
And I ask myself will it ever end?
The fields are bare, in fact so bare that they look
As if they've just been ploughed.

The cows are standing there looking at each other,
I wonder what they're thinking about?
They're probably saying to themselves
"Where's my bloody mate?"
Or something to that effect!

The winter sun is trying its best
To give us warmth,
But it's a lost cause really.
I must say there is a certain beauty
About those winter colours.
Even the sea looks different,
A touch of green, perhaps.

So what is the answer to a winter's tale?
May I suggest you get indoors,
Put on a fire,
And hibernate with a glass
Of something strong.
And that, my friend,
Should put an end
To a winter's tale.

THE SKY ROAD BLUES

If you ain't got the Sky Road blues
You ain't got nothing.
Go on, man, get yourself up that hill,
Walk, run, cycle or drive,
But just get up there.

Now that you are there, what do you see?
Hey, this is something else!
What a coastline this is,
And look at those islands
Dotted around the place.

That is the Atlantic ocean out there,
Yes, sir,
As far as the eye can see.
The next stop is the good old
US of A,
America to you, man!
If you want to swim
Three thousand miles
Be my guest.

Hey, folks, let's have those cameras clicking
This is the Sky Road
With castles, lighthouses,
deserted beaches and islands.
This is paradise and,
If you ain't got the Sky Road
blues by now,
You never will.

STAY LOOSE – STAY COOL

Yeah, man, stay loose stay cool.
Some will, some won't
Some can, some can't.
No hassle in the castle,
Just go with the flow.

Go slow, go fast - don't go at all!
It doesn't matter; sit down, lay down,
Or simply fall down - do it your way.
Don't blame anyone
Because it's all in the game.

Why worry? There is no hurry,
Snails don't, so I won't.
Listen, listen!
But I can't hear a thing.
Deafness perhaps?
Really old chap, how very strange.

Are you loose, are you cool?
Then go dude, go, shades on
Sing a song, dance a little,
Smile a lot,
Hey, you're a star!

Stay loose, stay cool,
That's the way to go,
Say hello, say hi,
But whatever you do
Don't be shy,
Get the message
What did I say?
I said stay loose,
Stay cool.

SIMPLICITY

Keep things simple, do, please do.
Complications bring stress
And more complexities. So what happens?
An emotional volcano, of course.

Embrace simplicity,
It's pure, simple and honest,
Simplicity is warm, caring, relaxing.
It's all around us – look for it.
Because it truly is there.

Nature is wonderful simplicity.
It gives you a universe of wonders.
Enjoy it because it is a feast of simplicity.
Gorge yourself on it.

Within ourselves there is an ocean of simplicity
Explore it, use it,
This vast pool of simplicity,
Drink it, inhale it,
Wrap it around you.

My fellow humans,
I ask you with all honesty,
Do not forsake simplicity
It is the core of happiness.

VANITY, VANITY

Vanity, vanity, always vanity,
Wherever we go, vanity goes.
In your sleep, in your dreams,
Vanity rules supreme.
Vanity is a mistress,
Vanity is a lover.

In the shops, in the stores, vanity lurks.
Oh yes! Vanity is waiting, buy me, please buy me,
I'm good for you, vanity whispers.
I'm in every bottle, you can't go wrong,
Just open me and see!
Wow! Don't I smell great? Go on, girl, buy me.
Yeah! I scored again.

Hey, girl, look at this outfit,
Wouldn't it look great on you?
Imagine yourself in the office, at a party.
Think about the looks you'll get,
The wolf whistles!
That's it girl, get your money out,
Great stuff! Vanity knows best.

Hang on, I see a guy over there,
Doesn't know what to buy.
Right mate, let's sort you out.
Can't make up your mind then, eh, old son?
So, when was the last time you pulled a girl?
Oh dear, oh dear, that long? Hmm!!
Right, try this shirt on - it's all the rage!
What about some hair gel?
There you go,
now you've got it.
You'll be fighting
the girls off tonight.

Vanity, Vanity.
We all need a bit of vanity.
So tomorrow is another day,
And vanity will make you pay.
So, goodbye from vanity,
See you soon.

WE ARE WHAT WE ARE

We are what we are.
We do what we do.
We say what we say.
It's a genetic thing.

Some are wise,
Some are foolish,
Some are brave,
Some are not,
But we are what we are.

I do this,
You do that,
They do something else,
We agree and disagree,
Such is the way of humanity.

People say this,
People say that,
Others will say
"Hey, is that a fact?"

All I say is:
Come what may,
We are what we are.

THE JOURNEY TO ENLIGHTENMENT

The journey to enlightenment
Is a long and lonely road
Littered with obstacles and temptations.
Many turn back half way there
Because they are not equipped
to take on board
The mountain of awareness
that confronts them.

I ask you to observe and listen.
Do you hear the birds singing?
Are they not happy and yet
They have no possessions
apart from the gift of flight?
We have everything but we want more,
Truly we are the spoilt children of the universe.

Look around you and what do you see?
Are you aware of the many happenings
that surround you?
Pause for a few moments.
And let the spirit of nature engulf you.
Let the wind caress your face.
Can you hear its whisper?
Unburden yourself, open your mind
And pass through the door
of enlightenment.
You will learn to tolerate and
understand all things.
You will acquire wisdom.
Cast aside your fear of the unknown,
Go on, I dare you!
Take the journey of enlightenment
And enter the world
of spiritual fulfilment.

SHIPS THAT PASS IN THE NIGHT

They pass each other in the night,
Bound for wherever,
No hellos, just a silent passing,
Darkness and ocean separates
one from the other.
Soon they are gone over the horizon,
Lights flickering as they sail into the night.

Are we not like those ships
That pass in the night,
Here today, gone tomorrow?
Is not life like the oceans,
Turbulent at times and calm at others?
How many of us have been shipwrecked?
Quite a lot I should imagine,
Were there enough lifeboats on board your ship,
Or did you have to swim to shore alone?

All of us are crew members
Of one ship or another,
Be it freighter or liner,
Perhaps sailing ship,
Even a speed boat,
Take your pick!
But one thing is paramount.
Is your ship sea worthy?
Is your crew fully fit
and at their posts?
Can your ship
take the pounding
of life's waves?
People, I will tell you now.
Life is the ocean
And we are the ships
That pass in the night.

PEDAL TO THE METAL

Rev, rev, rev, young hot rod drivers are raring to go,
Rev, rev, engines purring, impatience growing,
Chewing gum – the grid is cleared,
The lights say go.
They're off!

Screaming engines, burning rubber,
Every man for himself, crashes and smashes galore.
Gears changing, lots of swearing
It's pedal to the metal time
Lots of laps to go.

Who will survive? Time will tell.
Some will, some won't,
but what the hell.
It's bumps and thrills and spills.
Hey, this is the arena
of pedal to the metal,
Fewer cars now.

Drivers swerving in and out,
No quarter asked or given,
Oil and smoke everywhere,
One hundred and eighty
miles an hour or more.
The finishing line.

Zoom, zoom, zoom!
The first, second
and third past the flag,
A word with the winning driver.
Sir, what was it like out there?
"Hell man, pure hell,
But pedal to the metal wins every time."

NOBODY KNOWS WHY

Why do the birds fly?
And why does a child cry?
I guess nobody knows why!

Why do the seasons go round?
There must be a reason,
there must be.
Do we know why?
Does anybody know why?

Nature gives birth, flowers bloom,
The sun shines,
The rain falls,
Bees make honey,
Its beauty is boundless.
Do I know why?
No, I do not.
Do you know why?
I think nobody knows why!

The heavens are full of stars.
Look at them, please look!
They shine so bright,
only at night,
The moon becomes full.
Tides rise, oceans swell.
Why? I cannot tell,
I would ask you why,
But then nobody knows why.

All things must die,
Sad, so sad,
I wonder and I wonder.
Then I realise we are not numbers,
But don't ask me why,
Because all I can say is:
Nobody knows why,
Nobody knows why.

Hi, Johnny Cash, how do you do?
And my name ain't Sue,
I hear you drove fast cars
And sang in honky-tonk bars,
Through the rough and tumble,
You had a different point of view.

The guys in San Quentin
They said to give them a mention,
Yeah, they loved your show,
And they didn't have to
cough up any dough,
They were lucky man, real lucky.

Johnny Cash you really did
Walk the line – and fell into
That burning ring of fire
It seems nobody can stop
those flames
Getting higher and higher.

You know, Johnny Cash,
You gave us great memories,
And I guess no one like you
Will ever come again.
There are country singers,
And country singers,
But there is only one Johnny Cash.

Well, Johnny Cash,
I just want to say so long,
And thanks for all your songs.
Maybe you can put on a show
For the people in heaven,
After all, they're now your brethren.

So long partner,
So long Johnny Cash.

HOME IS WHERE YOUR HEART IS

What is home?
Home is that place where your heart is.
Home is a place of memories.
Home is a shrine to your childhood.
Home is Mum and Dad, brothers and sisters.
Home is all things to all people.

Home is where you can be yourself.
Home is your farm or land.
It's your pride and joy,
Just stand and look out across your fields.
You see your cows and sheep,
I bet your heart swells with pride.

Home is your little cottage,
Wherever it may be,
Perhaps beside the sea, who knows!
It may be humble,
But it is you,
It is your home.

Townhouse, city dwelling, apartment,
Each of them home.
Your home, my home,
Who can say which of us are alone
When we are at home?
Castles, river boats,
caravans, all homes.
From the humble to the mighty,
So it is fair to say,
Home is where your heart is.

HELLO – GOODBYE

Hellos are happy and can be fun.
Goodbyes are sad and full of pain.
Hello holds out promise
Goodbye is full of uncertainty.

I will smile when
I say hello.
I will try not to cry
When I say goodbye,
But all the time
I know I will.

At the first hello there is wonder,
Excitement and hope,
Power and strength,
Energy flows through veins.
Nothing is impossible.

Then it's time to say goodbye.
A great sadness dwells in one's heart,
The journey back to emotional limbo
Is long and lonely.

The worlds between hello and goodbye
Are miles apart.

DEATH IS REAL – LIFE IS UNREAL

Death is real, oh so very real,
And it is most certain indeed.
Death is final, no appeals, no reprieve.
Death is real.

Life is unreal, uncertain, no guarantees.
Life is full of ups and downs, swings and roundabouts.
Life if a roller-coaster with thrills and spills.
Life is unreal.

Death has no care for wealth or poverty.
Death does not distinguish between rich or poor.
Death is neutral, without fear or favour.
Death is real.

Life can be happy, life can be sad.
You may pull strings, or maybe you can't.
Either way, I'm sure you will agree,
That life is unreal.

The verdict:
Death is real,
Life is unreal.

A GAME OF POOL

It's a simple game – or is it?
You put your marker down
And wait your turn,
Stomach churning while you sip your beer.

Pool shark at the table,
Dishing out punishment to
the unprepared,
Cue ball spot-on each time,
That skillful bastard never misses,
Slam, bang, wham,
Down those balls go.

Victims keep coming and going,
And my nerves are going even faster.
Hell man, I haven't got a hope!
But I'm a sucker for punishment.
I want to run,
But my instincts tell me to stay.

It's my turn now
And I'm shaking like a leaf.
I pull myself together
And make a decent break.
Yellow for me, and reds for a flash cue
Who has a huge grin on his face.

He pots three to my one,
But I like the odds against me,
It makes me feel better.
Well, I've got to slow him down,
So block, snooker, anything,
But just stop him!

Hey, I'm beginning to feel good,
My plan is to wear him down,
Unnerve him – and it's working.
Two balls left for each of us,
He pots one and so do I.
Final balls each.

He pots first, I've got to put my yellow down,
And I do!
I miss the black, but so does he, again.
It's make or break time,
And I do it!
I pot the black.

"Hey man," he says:
"You were lucky."
Yeah, I say, I guess I was
But that's what a game of pool is all about.

ANDY'S SUNFLOWERS

I saw them, oh yes I saw them!
What did I see? Andy's sunflowers,
That's what I saw!
I did indeed see Andy's sunflowers,
Beasts, giants, monsters.

I climbed over Andy's wall
And there they all were,
Tall and proud, big and colourful,
Staring at me with their eyes.

Andy heard a noise,
He turned and fired his twelve-bore,
But I wasn't slow, hahaha!
I wouldn't let myself be sprayed.

Andy's secret was out,
I jumped and ran,
Laughing out loud, I shouted
Catch me if you can!

Now I'm going to tell everyone
About Andy's sunflowers!

A JEALOUS MIND

So destructive is a jealous mind.
It makes sworn lovers angry and blind,
Evil tongues spitting out words of folly,
The seeds of destruction become fertile
In the soil of a jealous mind.

The roots of jealousy spread far and wide,
Entangling pure hearts.
Destroying the flowers of love,
It is a cancer, an all consuming monster.
Its appetite knows no bounds.
I beg you do not cross its path,
It is a fate worse than death.

Insecurity, doubt, suspicion,
These are the symptoms of a jealous mind.
Blindness to reason soon follows,
Decay sets in,
The soul becomes confused.
What is right?
What is wrong?
It cannot distinguish.
Corrosion of the spirit is not far off.
Ask me for a cure,
There is none, I say.
But wait, there is one,
It's hard to find,
Yet it is to be found.
Tell us, please tell us,
What is the remedy for a jealous mind?

Love, trust, purity of mind, heart and soul,
Honesty with oneself,
This medicine, taken in large doses,
Over a long period of time,
Has been known to cure the illness
Known as a jealous mind.

Beware:
Do not fall prey to that beast
We call 'A Jealous Mind'.

CYBER BABE JANE 2525 AD

Hi Jane,
You are my new creation, you are ever so lucky.
And Jane says:
"Why so, human John?"

Because, my dear Jane,
You will never know pain,
You will never know sorrow,
You are tomorrow.

I am the past.
You are the future.
You will walk, talk and laugh
Always.

Cyber Babe Jane,
You will never cry,
neither will you die,
I am mortal.
You are immortal.

Welcome to planet Earth,
Cyber Babe Jane.
Welcome to the place
Where you will forever remain.

SINGERS AND SONGS

Yeah, it's true, you know.
It's true that singers and songs
Always get along,
In fact, they are almost twins.

Great singers and great songs,
They go hand in hand.
Where one goes, so does the other.
Hey, have you ever tried wearing just one glove?
It doesn't work!
But singers and songs do.

Think of Sinatra, Dillon, Cash, Presley
And all the other great singers
With great songs.
No, not chalk and cheese,
But musicians such as these singers and songs.

Singers and songs,
Go ding-dong, ding-dong.
A perfect match, brilliant harmony,
A match made in heaven.

Listen to singers
and their songs
It's artistic manna.
Pure inspiration,
with no perspiration!
Natural rhythm
with perpetual motion.

Ladies and gentlemen, I can
promise you,
There is so much power,
So much energy,
In singers and songs.
Tap into it - before it evaporates!

MY INFINITE DREAM

She is my dream, my infinite dream,
To deny so would be folly.
In my soul and within my spiritual depths.
I know I must cherish my dream,
Because she is my infinite dream.

Her eyes, her smile, set me on fire.
I want to move mountains and earth,
And I shall if she so desires,
Such is the power and strength of my dream.

You, my darling, are the core of my world,
You are the power that drives the engine
Of my infinite dream,
And it must never fail, never ever fail.

My dream will travel on, and on, and on,
Through the cosmos and through the universe
It will travel,
It is infinite.
It is my infinite dream.

If my dream should die,
Then I will surely cry,
And broken hearts rarely mend.
But this will not happen,
Because, my love,
You are my infinite
dream.

CLIFDEN – MY HOME TOWN

A town, yes!
But not like any other town I know,
That's Clifden – my home town.
It's a small place, rather cute, quaint,
I'm happy whenever I come here.
I feel a sense of belonging.
And there are some wonderful characters living here,
I can't name them all of course,
But God bless them all.

There are pubs, lots of them,
Each with its own atmosphere.
Do visit these ale houses if you come to Clifden,
I guarantee you won't be disappointed.
And the music – wow!
Traditional of course, and other styles.
The art shops, coffee shops and restaurants,
So many – and all of them great.

Are you a betting person?
Then please do visit the betting shop.
It's a treat, believe me, it's a treat.
Horses on TV screens, oh, and people.
There is something for everyone.
And, speaking of people,
Do seek out one Thomas Lyden,
Poet and master punter – he cannot lose!

So there you have it, folks,
That's Clifden – my home town.

A CITY GARDEN

Sitting here in this city garden,
With so many colourful
Flowers and trees,
Protected by sturdy walls.

The city outside is all hustle and bustle,
But this garden is so peaceful.
Butterflies chase each other,
Birds are singing
To their heart's content,
Chirp! Chirp! Chirp!
They make such lovely music.

Those trees look so strong,
With their plumage of leaves
and blossoms,
I can't resist touching them.
There are a few bumble bees flying around,
Collecting nectar I suspect.

It's so beautiful in this city garden,
You can gather your thoughts.
In a sanctuary such as this,
The sun is beaming down,
And don't those flowers just love it?
Tulips and roses with their petals opened wide,
They are swaying gently in the summer breeze.
I wonder if heaven would be like this?

THE SEA FROM MY WINDOW

I just sit here and gaze out to sea,
It's the Atlantic, of course,
And I wonder to myself
What it would be like to sail
Into the vast yonder single-handed,
Battling those huge waves.
They are angry and want to punish me
For intruding upon their watery domain.

The fierce wind tearing at sails,
Whipping at my face and limbs,
But I will not give in to the elements.
It's time for a stout heart
And nerves of steel.

Mountainous waves are tossing me about,
And survival is paramount.
It is so dark and lonely
And I pray that I will survive this night.
A quote from somewhere
comes into my mind.
Yes, that's it:
'Lonely are the brave'
Well, right now I am awfully alone,
And I'm trying to be brave.

Another huge wave is charging in,
The spraying seas across my bow.
It seems to go on and on.

Will this night ever end?
It doesn't appear so,
But it will soon be dawn
And maybe calmer waters.
I can't help making the comparison
Between the sea and life.
One day it's calm, the next, turbulent.
The sun is breaking through the clouds.
The sea is subdued,
And it's calm waters ahead.

Even the dolphins have arrived
to greet me.
Right now I feel great, elated even.
So change the sails,
Grab the helm,
And sail into the vast horizon.

I just remembered.
I'm only daydreaming.

INNER BEAUTY

In this mundane humdrum life
You tread quietly through
all its strife,
Content with your inner
thoughts,
And not over battles others fought,
But rather friendships
and loves you sought.

Your beauty is both outer and inner,
Rare qualities indeed,
What lovely place do you enter,
In the confines of your mind, pray tell,
That we may cease to be blind
And share with you this heaven you find?

Creativity and inner peace is your desire,
Not for you the suffering of fools,
Trapped in their seas of conflict.
It is for you to transcend to higher planes,
Fuelled by your inner-beauty, you will shine.
Like a beacon you will glow
In the world of darkness.

They will mock you, they will laugh and snigger,
But you shall not be harmed.
Inner beauty is your strength and armour,
It will guide you through the battlefields of mortal man.
You have the universe with you,
You have inner beauty.

LOVE IS A BEAUTIFUL THING

Love is, and always will be, a beautiful thing.
As in the past and in the future
Love will flourish, love will triumph,
Love will conquer.

Love is like a summer rose,
With its soft scented petals
Opened and in full bloom.
It is beautiful,
Just as love is a beautiful thing.

To deny love is to deny life,
Because love is the fuel of life.
Without it the spirit and soul
Would die.

When I observe a loving couple
It is like magic, they seem to float
And there is a warmth about them.
Hence my saying,
Love is a beautiful thing.

Love goes round and round and round.
It knocks on our doors
not twice or thrice,
But many times,
So don't shut it out, just invite it in.

Love is perpetual,
Love is resplendent,
Love is strong,
Powerful and potent,
Love is a beautiful thing.

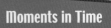

THE WALK OF ENCHANTMENT

It is not just any walk.
It is that final walk,
The one known as the walk
of enchantment.
Once you are called you cannot say no,
You must go and walk alone.
Remember bring only thyself,
No one but thyself.

Be you rich or poor, prince or pauper,
It matters not, take no coin or cash.
There is no need of such earthly things,
For the walk of enchantment is short and beautiful.
You will meet other walkers along the way,
But you will not speak.
You will be without worries or troubles,
Life's problems will no longer be with you.

You will see valleys covered in flowers,
And lakes full with crystal clear water,
Animals of all kinds,
And drink from gentle sweet waters.
There will be no envy or anger,
Just warmth and contentment.
A flight of white doves will constantly fly overhead,
All is calm and peaceful.

And now you are near the end
Of the walk of enchantment,
A bright light beckons, its glow is so soft and warm.
All will pass through its rays
And into the domain beyond.

All will be cleansed,
Never again to suffer the burdens of mortal life.
So ends the walk of enchantment.
And all that I say will come to pass.

LOST IN THE SEA OF MADNESS

Troubled mind, tormented soul forever lost,
Lost in the sea of madness.
But why? How?
Once there was happiness, contentment and friends,
Now, they are gone, all gone.
This sea of madness is so deep, so cold,
There is no light,
Just an infinity of darkness.

This sea of madness is so full;
Cries of anguish are all around me,
Strange creatures beckon, laughing.
"We've got you, we've got you all,
Foolish humans!
We are the masters of the sea of madness
And you shall suffer all manner of torments!
This is the place of demons,
They dwell here in their thousands,
Do you not know you have entered the sea of madness?"

No, no, please listen to me,
I don't belong here,
There must be some mistake, I am innocent!
I have not committed any offence!
"Oh, but you have, my dear foolish human,
You have indeed offended.
Did you not fill your body with strange substances
And continue to do so?
Yes, of course it was fun,
But now you are here
In the sea of madness."

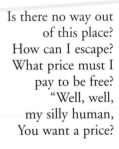

Is there no way out
of this place?
How can I escape?
What price must I
pay to be free?
"Well, well,
my silly human,
You want a price?

Ha! Ha! of course
I will tell you my price!
Your soul - that is my price."
No, please, I can't sell you my soul,
Anything else, but not my soul!
"Very well, if you insist,
I, the master of the sea of madness,
Am prepared to release you
from this place,
But if you return here again,
You lose your soul to me.
Mark my words, human:
You will give your soul to me,
Now, go quickly.
Go, foolish human.
Go from this sea of madness."

THERE ARE RAINBOWS IN THE DARK

Yes indeed, there are rainbows in the dark.
But where, where? I hear you ask.
Oh, you must look, look and look again,
Because there are rainbows in the dark.

Find them, find them, please find them!
Find the rainbows in the dark.
They are so beautiful, so brilliant,
Such colours, just glowing in the dark.

Is it a dream, or are they real?
Ask me how I feel,
And I will say with zeal,
That there are rainbows in the dark.

Open your eyes, open them wide.
Now search, search, search!
Search for the rainbows in the dark.
They are there, truly they are there.

When you find them they will glow,
Only then will you know,
That you have found the holy grail.
Did I not say, there are rainbows in the dark?

THE WORLD OF SILENCE

Silence is golden.
True, how very true.
Will you enter with me now
Into the world of silence?
Silence is still,
Silence is deep,
Silence is an ever flowing river.
Onwards and downwards it flows,
Silence beckons us to follow its winding path.

Listen.
Listen to the silence.
Let it engulf you, have no fear, there is no pain.
Let silence speak to you.
Are you of troubled mind?
Then bathe in the waters of silence.
Is it not soothing? Banish those worries,
Fly on the wings of silence,
Breath in the freedom of silence.

Meditate, contemplate,
Cleanse your mind, cleanse your soul.
Let your spirit loose,
Unlock your chains of imprisonment.
Now you are free,
Free to travel in the world of silence.
Isn't it beautiful?
Isn't it wonderful?
Leave behind your anger and frustration!

You can visit the world of silence
as often as you like.
There is no charge, no restrictions,
You can wander without hindrance,
Let me leave you with this quote:

'Listen to the music of silence,
For when the music stops
The silence is deafening.'

SPEAK TO ME OF LOVE

If you speak to me of love,
I shall tell you of highs and lows
Of passion and depression.

Love may be true, love may be false
With doubts about doubts.
Yes, do speak to me of love
And I'll raise my eyes to the man above.

Moments of happiness
Followed by moments of sadness.
Oh, why must it be so?
Indeed, do speak to me of love.

Did you ever swim in the sea of love?
Were you tossed about
By its mighty waves?
Yes, do speak to me of love.

Speak to me of love
And I'll remember walking
hand in hand
Over the sand, my, my.
But those were the days
of wine and roses.

Please, please, speak to me of love,
Speak to me of love.

MOMENTS IN TIME

How long is a moment in time?
Some say it is a lifetime,
You can debate this point, of course,
I say a moment in time is a capsule,
A millisecond in the sphere of infinite time.

There are moments, moments and moments,
Tiny moments of our lives.
Once they pass they cannot be relived.
I suspect there is a hidden library somewhere,
A place where all our moments are stored.

For instance:
A moment of anger
Followed by a moment of regret,
Too late to change, gone forever.
A moment of despair,
When all seems lost
And no-one cares,
Pray to him who does.
A moment of sheer bliss as lovers kiss,
A moment of embrace,
Such sweet rapture,
A moment of pride as a mother holds
Her newborn child,
The moment of creation is alive.

A look, a thought, a smile.
A blink of an eye,
They all occur in a moment in time.
Great empires have come and gone,
They, too, were but moments in time.

In parting, let me say this:
Our very lives are just moments in time.

IF ONLY

If only they had love
Instead of a leather glove,
Their smiles would have
Melted hard hearts.

If only little boys' tears
Could be stored.
What a well of sorrow
To drink from.

If only there were open arms
To shelter in.
But no, no, no,
Only pain and tears.
No-one to understand so many fears.

And yet, they played
As children do.
Laughter stopped
When the whistle blew.
Lights out meant refuge for the night.

Oh, how I wish you were able
To witness such sights.
My heart forgives,
But in my memory they still live.

If only.
If only.
If only.

About the Poet

John Dunne is a product of the industrial school system - he is a 'Letterfrack boy' - but his industrial school experience was unusual. Unlike most others, John was only four years old when he entered the system. On Wednesday, 2nd June 1948, John was sentenced by the District Court to be detained at Letterfrack Industrial School, to remain there until the day before his sixteenth birthday, 29th May, 1960.

In 1950 there were 51 Industrial Schools dispersed across Ireland, in which a total of 6000 children were detained. All run by religious orders, the largest was Artane, in Dublin, which held 776 boys. Opened in 1887, Letterfrack, in Co. Galway, eventually held 150 boys, who were taught by the Congregation of Christian Brothers. It closed in 1973.

According to the document which sent John to Letterfrack, (called an 'Order of Detention in a Certified Industrial School' *see inside back cover*), he was dispatched there upon information from an NSPCC official that he had been found 'having a parent who does not exercise proper guardianship'. Once there, John was among scores of other boys who had been sentenced in a similar way for a huge variety of reasons. These included petty crimes and simple 'mitching' - school absenteeism.

In recent years, allegations of abuse within the institutions began to surface, directed at the harsh regime operated by the Christian Brothers at Letterfrack Industrial School and others. A five year-long Garda investigation into alleged physical and sexual abuse of boys in his care resulted in one former Letterfrack Brother receiving a lengthy custodial sentence. Mr. Justice Séan Ryan was appointed Chair of the Commission to Inquire into Child Abuse. Established by statute in 2000, evidence of abuse was heard from over a thousand individuals in private sittings, and separate public hearings were held in respect of each institution.

The State made a formal apology to victims of such abuse.

> **"**
> I didn't know what family life was like so I didn't really miss it
> **"**

Recognising the extent and seriousness of the problem, a 'Redress Board' was set up under the Residential Institutions Redress Act 2002, to make awards of money to people who, as children, were abused while resident in industrial schools and other institutions subject to state regulation or inspection.

The victims of abuse have been affected in different ways. Peter Tyrrell, another Letterfrack boy, but of the 1920s and 30s, wrote extensively and vividly of his experiences, although the manuscript lay unpublished for half a century. Tyrrell set fire to himself on Hampstead Heath, London, in 1967. The manuscript was later discovered by Diarmuid Whelan, who edited it, and it was finally published by Irish Academic Press under the title *Founded on Fear*, in 2006. Others, unable to find a means by which to deal with the trauma, have had to remain silent.

John Dunne, the poet, seldom dwells upon the subject of his Letterfrack experiences. His intensely personal and moving *If Only (page 89)* is the only poem in this collection to touch on them directly. With due irony, John feels he was perhaps lucky to have been sent to Letterfrack when he was only four. He says, "It meant I didn't really know what family life was like, so I didn't really miss it. The school was my home, it was all I knew."

The story that follows is, of course, true. It is John Dunne's account of his brief life before industrial school, the years spent under the oppressive regime of the Christian Brothers and an insight into his later influences. John is at once an eccentric, a comedian, and a self professed clown. He is though, a consummate entertainer and performer, delighting crowds with regular readings of his work at *Basket House*, Clifden. Just as John is fiercely proud of being a Letterfrack boy, I too am extremely proud that he calls me a friend.

Ben Crow
Claddaghduff 2007

(Above) Letterfrack Industrial School c1920 *(Photo: Courtesy Letterfrack Furniture College)*

A Letterfrack Boy

"My mother was from Yorkshire in England, and was in service at a grand house called Ballinaboy Lodge, near Clifden, for many years. I met a woman recently who remembered working with my mother. She described her as a 'real rebel'! My father lived nearby in a small cottage. He was tall, tanned and weather-beaten. They fell in love, I was a product of that love, and here I am to tell the tale. I don't know what happened, but they split up when I was four and I was sent to St Joseph's Industrial School, Letterfrack. I was there for eleven years. I was unusual - I spent the whole of my childhood there, from the age of four until I was sixteen. Other boys came at all sorts of ages - six, ten, twelve - any age. We all left at sixteen. I soon learnt never to think or question, but of course I know now that we were all ordered there by the courts.

I remember my first day at St Joseph's. I stood all alone in what seemed to me to be a vast hall. I didn't know why I was there and it didn't dawn on me that I wouldn't see my mother again for years, or that I wasn't going home again.

I feel very proud to have been a Letterfrack boy because it meant I learnt to be self-reliant and independent. I was disciplined and single-minded. St Joseph's was my life and my home. I learnt to always keep a stiff upper lip and never to show my feelings. I think I owe much of my inventiveness and creativity to how I was brought up at Letterfrack.

I think I was lucky in a way, because I was only four when I went to Letterfrack. I had no experience of home or family life. It was perhaps less damaging for me because I hadn't formed that bond that you have with your parents at that stage.

There were about twenty boys to a dormitory. On a typical day we would rise at 6.30am. The monk in charge would only have to enter the dormitory and we'd quickly jump out of bed. The first thing was to get washed. Afterwards, we would shine the floors of the dormitory and the washing area. We lined up on our hands and knees with a cloth and would work our way from one end to the other. When the monk decided we had finished the floors, he would blow a whistle and we'd be able to get up and put away the polishing equipment and walk smartly down to the main yard.

In the yard we would be lined up like a military unit. An older boy would count us, and say that we were all present to the monk in charge. Then we'd walk in twos up to church for morning mass at 7.30am. We filed into church and I remember sitting on the right hand side with all the other boys from my dormitory. Mass would last for half an hour, and the monk in charge would sit behind us to watch over us. The other monks would sit in a separate section of the church. I loved mass. It was my comfort and my sanctuary - it was private time. I felt a sense of serenity and peace, it felt as though I had actually a mother when I was in mass. In many ways I felt religion was my mother. The religious aspects of life at Letterfrack are what enabled me to get through it.

When mass was over, we walked down to the hall and had breakfast. We sat seven or eight to a table. We always sat by the same people - I looked on the place where I sat as my place, where no-one else could sit. The breakfast, perhaps porridge, was already there on the table for us when we got there. Some of the older boys had the job of taking it to the tables before we arrived.

Before we ate, grace was said by the monk in charge, who would be sitting on a high stool watching us. It was always the same monk. We had tea, and sometimes had a slice of bread and jam. I always thought we had enough - mind you, I was very thin!

At nine o'clock, we were off to lessons in the classroom. We always kept to the same groups as a class, moving as a unit to a different classroom each term. It was very difficult to learn because of the fear factor - the fear of getting a question wrong, or looking dissentful. We had basic lessons in the three Rs, as well as religious lessons. The monk taking the lesson would stand at the front and, if we got a question wrong, we would be punished. Sometimes the local parish priest came in and tested us on the catechism. He'd ask a boy a question from the catechism, and if he got it wrong his name would be taken. The monks dealt with the boy later - his giving a wrong answer was a slur on the monk's teaching. I was always very good at the catechism and never got any questions wrong.

The type of punishment depended upon the monk in question. They all carried a leather strap in their robe pockets. The strap was two or three layers of stiff leather, beautifully sewn together, with a handle at one end. It was about eighteen inches long and reminded me of a roman soldier's short sword.

> ❝ The strap was two or three layers of stiff leather beautifully sewn together ❞

Punishment could be six or seven strokes of the strap, on the hand or on the backside. It seemed to me that this was given almost at random, and no-one knew what the boy concerned had done to deserve punishment. Perhaps it was for showing dissent, looking rebellious, misbehaving in class, being found smoking or just getting a question wrong - or perhaps just because the monk had taken a dislike to him. I got the strap several times myself, and while I can't remember what for, I can certainly remember the feeling of the hard leather strap on a cold winter's morning!

We just shook off the punishments. It hurt alright, but it was as meaningful to us as having a slice of bread. The motto was 'don't think or question, just do'. I sometimes wondered to myself why I was there, but I suppressed the thought - it was for the best.

Lessons broke at lunchtime, about half past one, which marked the end of school for the day, and we went into the hall for a meal. Like all other meals, dinner was conducted in silence, or perhaps in low whispers, under the watchful eye of the monk in charge on his high stool. I remember the meals as being adequate, with home grown vegetables, meat and potatoes, or perhaps soup. Anyone who failed to eat their food was punished with the strap by the monk in charge.

I had a number of friends of roughly the same age, and we met up at break times. We talked about things like who'd been punished and what was happening that day. We never discussed anything that could lead to talking about our feelings - such as why we were there or what we thought of the school. Like we did in private, we simply suppressed these thoughts - to do otherwise would be to allow our feelings to come to the surface. Again, we didn't think or question, we just 'did'.

After dinner, at about two thirty, we lined up in our same groups and went to our work stations. This would be working on the farm, in the greenhouse, the carpenter's workshop, or as in my case, the knitting room. I loved the work in the knit-

> **I took myself off to another place in my day-dreams**

ting room. There was a lady in charge, one of only four women, I think, who included housekeepers for the monks and a nurse. We sewed jumpers and darned socks for the boys and made up sheets. We had to make so many each day, and while we didn't get punished, the lady in charge certainly shouted at us if we weren't working fast enough.

At about five thirty, when work for the afternoon was over, we re-assembled in the yard and went to the hall for tea. As usual, the monk in charge supervised us from on high while we ate bread and jam and drank tea. Afterwards there would be catechism lessons. The monk taking the lesson would tell stories and we were expected to learn the catechism word perfect. We also had homework on the catechism which we would be expected to do by ourselves in the dormitory later.

As I said, I was very good at the catechism - I felt happy and comforted by it. I was secretly proud of being good at it too.

Later, there would be some free time in the dormitory, followed by lights out at eight thirty or nine o'clock. A monk would come in, switch the lights off and shout 'lights out!' and I would lie and day-dream - perhaps about being a cowboy. I think this was how my creativity first manifested itself in me - I took myself off to another place in my daydreams.

I was quite inventive, too. Once, I took the clockwork motor out of a tinplate toy car and put it into an aeroplane I'd made out of pieces of cardboard. The propeller was an ice-cream stick - it really worked and went careering off across the yard! I was always thought of as being a bit eccentric.

At weekends, the routine varied a little, and on Saturdays there would be no school. We'd go to our work stations after mass and breakfast in the morning. Later, we sometimes went into Ellis Hall to watch a film. These were always a high point and we eagerly anticipated going to the films. On Sundays, after mass, the monks often took us on long walks, maybe to Kylemore or Tully. Having walked all the way there, we would simply turn around and walk back again. One of the good things I remember about weekends was that we were able to have a shower.

From a very early age, I remember reading newspapers and everything else I could lay my hands on. I was intrigued by words and, while I didn't have access to a dictionary, I loved the sounds they made in my head.

I left the classroom at the age of fourteen, after I'd sat the Primary Certificate examination. We'd learnt most things by rote - we chanted out spellings in class - that's how I learnt best. Memory was king, and my memory was very good.

At fourteen, I went to work full time on the school's farm. Farm work involved working full time from nine o'clock until five thirty, doing all the jobs necessary to keep the farm running smoothly, to enable the school to be self sufficient. I loved this work and the fact that there were only six of us together. There would be milking the

cows, sewing and harvesting pota-toes, saving the hay and tending the land. We were still supervised - every moment of my life at the industrial school was supervised until the day I left - but on the farm there was only a lay supervisor. While he had the power of punishment, he was not regarded with as much fear as the monks.

I only saw my mother once while I was at Letterfrack. One day I was told she was there, waiting to see me in the yard. I was about eleven then, and a monk told me to go down and see her. I remember this lady in front of me. I had a vague idea that we were connected, but I couldn't really work out who she was, or why she was there. We didn't make any contact at all and I remember the silence between us. I don't think I spoke, and I can't remember anything she said to me. I didn't feel anything towards her apart from this vague connection. I didn't cry - this wasn't allowed in my approach to life. She left, and I felt proud that I could handle it.

Every year, I was released for four weeks, and went home to my father's house in Ballinaboy. My father came to school about a month before, to sign the release papers. I had to sign them too, and this would be the first time I'd know that 'holidays' were near.

The cottage in Ballinaboy was a typical country cottage. Three rooms, whitewashed outside, with a grey galvanised roof. The door was dark brown, and you went straight into the kitchen, the main room of the house. There was the usual big fireplace to the left, which was where all the cooking was done, and a big table in the middle of the room, always with a table cloth on it. Opposite the door stood a big dresser, on which there were lots of decorative plates - but I also remember lots of delicate, flowery chinaware and a teapot. There were tiny egg cups in the same pattern too! Everything else was purely practical - the floor was just concrete, no lino or rugs.

I really looked forward to the fantastic sense of freedom that being released would bring. For a whole month, I could run across the fields, down to the lake or anywhere I wanted! I really dreaded going back to school at the end of the month. It took several weeks to adjust back to being constantly supervised and being afraid of the strap. But, like everything else, you just did it. It was just what you had to do - you certainly didn't question it.

I suppose the school's aim was to prepare boys for a life of work outside, after we'd left. When the day came for me to leave when I was sixteen, the first I knew of it was that one day I was told to pack my things - there was a car waiting outside to take me to Ballynahinch Castle!

I was overjoyed to be leaving, especially as I was going to work at Ballynahinch. I was given a letter to give to the manager of the Castle and off I went. Even after I'd been in their charge for twelve years, not one of the monks came to wish me luck or say goodbye.

Arriving at Ballynahinch, I gave my letter to the hotel manager, ironically a Miss Dunne, who outlined my duties and her expectations of me. She made it very clear to me that I was to receive no days off, but that I was to get up early each day, shine all the guests' shoes, cut and carry logs for the fires and take the suitcases of arriving and departing guests to and from their rooms.

Otherwise, I would be in the kitchen washing up or scrubbing the floors - in fact anything the occasion demanded. I was a general dog's body - but I didn't mind, I was away from Letterfrack and in relative paradise. I was always on duty, but I had wonderful meals and a degree of freedom I had never before experienced, as well as thirty shillings a week in my pocket. I was also given a very smart collar and tie, and a pink fez to wear!

I soon realised that my time at Ballynahinch was as a result of an arrangement that the castle, and other hotels and willing businesses in the area, had with the industrial school. They would take leaving boys like me for a set period of two years, after which my time was up, and I had to move on so that another boy could replace me on leaving the school.

Miss Dunne gave me an excellent reference, and I found a job in Wicklow doing similar work. When I was old enough I went into the army. This seemed a natural move to me - many other industrial school boys did the same. Having been brought up in a semi-militaristic way at school, I found life in the army quite comfortable and rewarding.

It was many years later that I found a way to express my artistic feelings through these poems. Painters paint pictures - words are my paintings. There is a universe within words."